# T H I S

# MOUTH

▲▲▲

## Text by Alan Whitaker
## Photographs by Paul Gay

This mouth eats weeds.

Ducks eat weeds.

This mouth eats seeds.

A finch eats seeds.

# This mouth eats grass.

A sheep eats grass.

# This mouth eats nectar.

A moth eats nectar.

# This mouth eats leaves.

A giraffe eats leaves.

# This mouth eats meat.

A dog eats meat.

13

# This mouth eats fish.

A shark eats fish.

This mouth eats ice cream.

I eat ice cream!